This book belongs to:

_____

Find 4

Make a Match

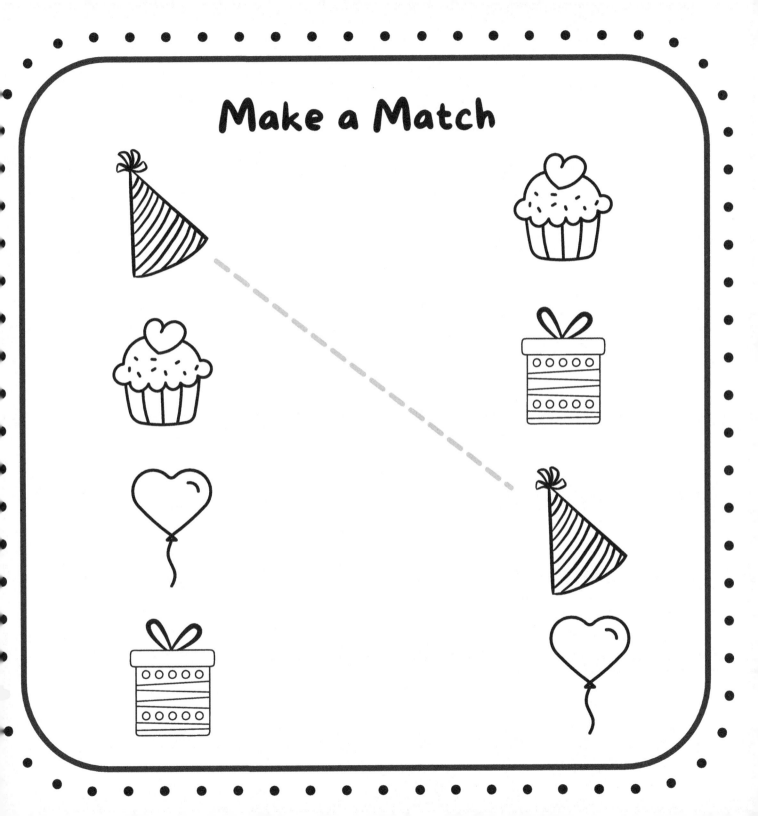

I am 4

My name is

Count and Match

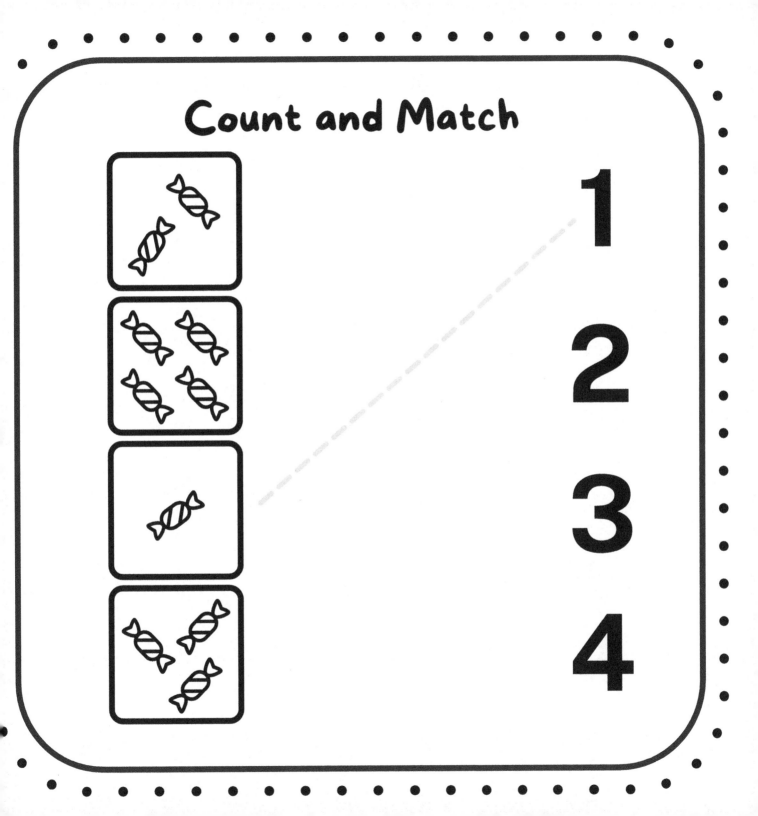

Trace the lines to make the number 4

I am 4

My favorite colors are

Trace the lines to help the friends find their toys.

Circle the groups of 4

Rainbow write the number 4.
Trace the number with 4 colors.

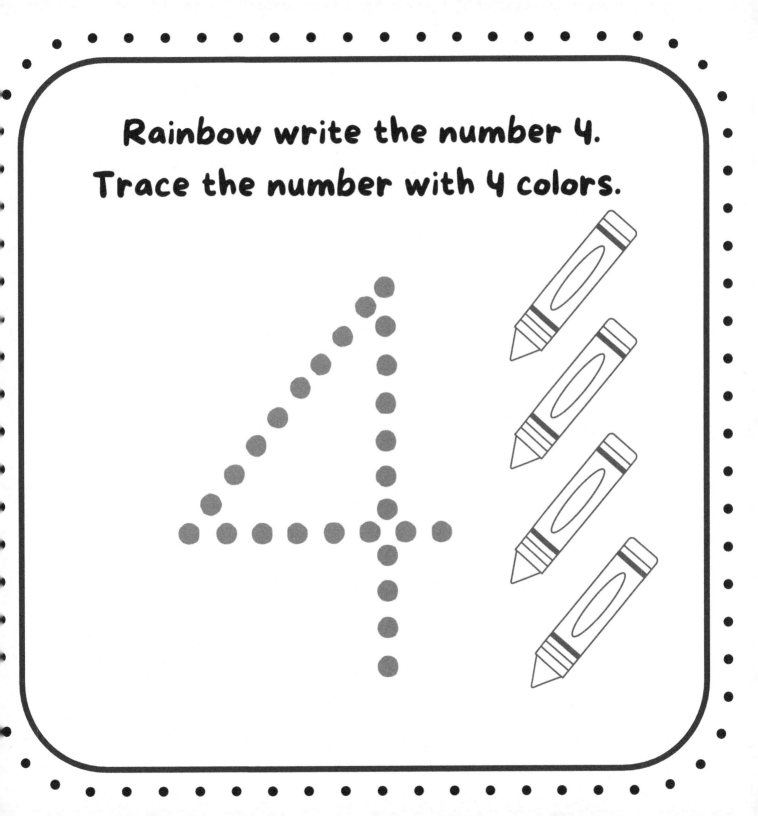

Count and Color

Make a Match

I am 4

My favorite foods are

Count and Match

1
2
3
4

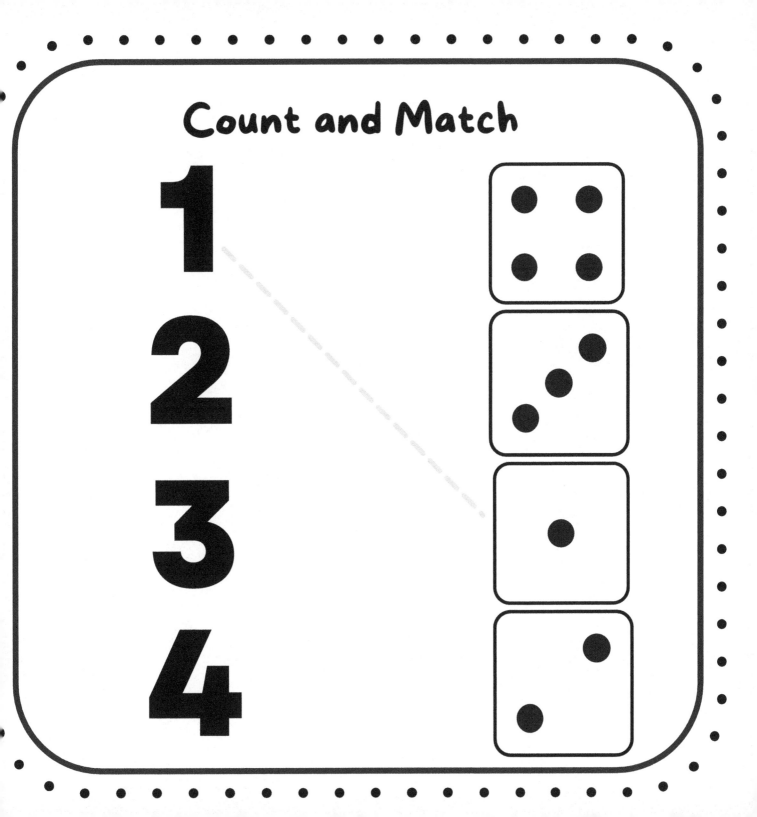

Trace the numbers.
Match the number to the butterflies.

1 2 3 4

Go through the maze to get all 4 cupcakes.

I can draw

Trace the circle and draw a happy face.

Find 4

Follow the trail to help the friends get their treats.

Go through the maze to get all 4 ladybugs.

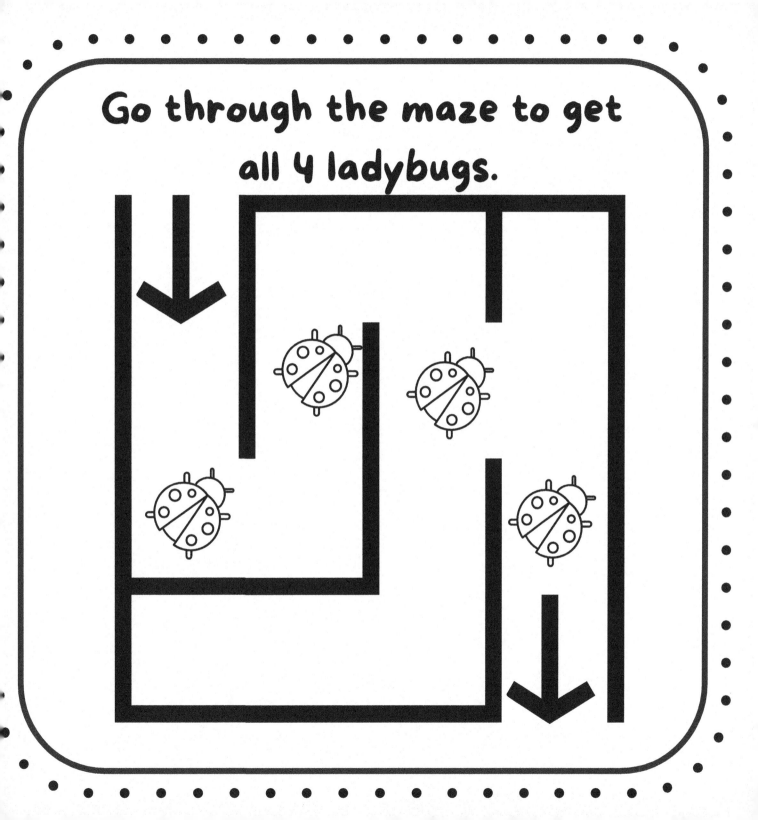

I am 4

I can draw a picture.

Made in United States
Orlando, FL
13 June 2023

34065578R00057